Dedicated

About The Author

Tina lives at her Home in The West Midlands, with her two Son's and two Dogs, Milo and Kenny.

She is openly on the Autistic Spectrum and very proud to acknowledge the fact she has Asperger's Syndrome. Prior to this Tina has published to date five Books. For more details:

> Website: tinajcoxpoetry.com
> instagram: Tina_J_cox
> Facebook: @Tinajcoxpoetry
> Twitter: @tinajcoxpoetry

I would like to thank David Wakelam of ETC Photographics for designing the Book Cover to The Truth :)

> "Keep shining in a World that is all too dark at times.
> Your Light is precious"

Much Love

Tina J. Cox xx

Contents

My World

The Skies Blue & Red with Clouds of Neon
Beauty lasts indefinitely, maybe an Eon
Reality is down to perception, imagination
It's an invention of both Mind & Creation
Life, is a Black & White Movie on Screen
Of Gut wrenching scenes, tearing out Spleen
To those scenes played out, that I don't mind
Remembering that Memories are imaginary
For entertainment & merely fragmentary
A past only for me, for you a Story to be told
My existence is unclear, but it will unfold
All that I ever was & indeed will ever be
Defined in time, as a Moment for me
Emotions are decoded as real & physical
For example Love, now, that is one typical
Each of us, is born alone destined for a Journey
Before dying alone, destined for a Gurney
A life of stark visionary Illusion & Touch
The emotions are at best help & a Crutch

Traitors

"Hello, I need to see you,
it's been to long overdue,
there is an attraction,
that is a BIG distraction.
Do you sense it?
It's biting at the Bit"

"They don't suspect?"
"No, I kinda checked.."

"Where, that Coffee Place?"
"Yeah, sounds ace!"

"Sure you want this later?"
"Yes, though I feel a Traitor"

"But this needs to be resolved"
(God, I so want to be involved)

"Text me when you get away..."
"You mean, when I come out to play?..."
Giggles "Don't be so sure"
"Relax, my thoughts are pure!"

(My Body aches on the inside)
(Guilt hits like an incoming Tide)

"Yeah, later's" say the Traitor's.

Myself

I have hardly any reason to wake
Any purpose, is mine to take
I am older & wiser, a born again
Love run's through my main vain
It's broken & continuous
Contradicting & unjust

Most Night's I retreat into my solace
To a corner of Mind, that is spotless
To think & ponder on the 'what if's'
Uncertainties & life's little 'squiff's'
Alone, I can't do anyone any harm
Just in 'my World' & feeling calm

My Sub-Conscious is never at rest
It's active & constantly under test
What would it be, to silence my Mind?
Perhaps cruel, unjust & quite unkind
Perhaps this is why I am lonely....
That the only Person, I need is me

Bondage

Welcome to the Bondage, I call Mind
You don't have to stay or even be kind
Manipulate, shout & treat me cruelly
Just to let me shout back, unruly
Take the time, to search my idea's
That I share with you, not my Peers
Put them into your blackened Heart
Before stabbing & tearing me apart
Then choke me with your Fire & Flame
Over & over, until with excitement, came
Repentance is not an option neither
The choice to leave isn't there either
Imprisoned by the shackles of Time
The Hands of Demon's grab to climb
We have clung to The Cross for so long
For it ever to feel and be wrong
We will not look at God without t'uther
I know we will hold Hands & blubber
Don't let my Hand go at Death's Door
I couldn't think to go on any more
So, we will go on and live in this limbo
Limbs & Flesh, hanging, all akimbo
For an entirely different World exists
Between your verbal abuse & Fist's.

Youth

So young and uninspired
My expectation had expired
A desire to be protected
To a degree, directed
I needed you for something
It should've been a Fling
Everything and I wanted more
Problems ate us to the Core
....and it was better we parted
after they started...
I still don't quite know
Apart from all the Sorrow
The odd loving moment
Mixed with being opponent
I was addicted to 'different'
It was actually, ignorant
The Curse of my Youth
I'm confronting the Truth
We would work, I insisted
If only they hadn't persisted
But, I was beyond stubborn
So convinced I could govern
I made my Bed & on it, I lied
Played my Cards & then cried
Though not all in total vain
I have a good life in the main
Thank you for 'whatever'
All the Ties we cannot sever

Nan

Nan is wonderful and Nan is kind
She is in my Heart, I think you will find
That won't change with the time passing
So many loving thoughts, keep amassing
She takes everything in her Stride
She is the slow oncoming Tide
My Mother, Sister, Friend & Nan
She does everything she possibly can
She is glorious & I am proud
That you are you & I say it aloud.

Surrounded

I feel your omnipresence surrounding
..my Skin and the fresh air is pounding
Every Raindrop that falls contains you
Your handsome, friendly, smiling Face
Still empty Handed, after giving chase
Your warmth soaks me to the Bone
I will not forget, while hear alone
Memories chill and I want more Rain
The last Meeting hurt, so much Pain
A broken Woman, pieced fragmental
Moral Compass was down, accidental
I lay down and shiver inside, resigned
When it rains over me, I'm inclined
I am thankful, that you were my Friend
Albeit, not quite to the very end
I pray for Storms to hold you close
When time stands still, together froze

My Storm

Hold onto my Hand, in the Slipstream
This is not real, it's a tragic Dream
The Hurricane circles us & roars
We stand in the Middle, I am yours
Hold me to you, while I cup your Face
Adrenaline is making the Heart race
All the moments grabbed lead to this
A passionate embrace & stolen Kiss
A complexity of emotions so haunting
In a desolate landscape so daunting
Under Fist in a tightly fitted Glove
We are beautiful & so in Love
The Pendulum swings ominously
Yet somehow decides honourably
Time is for us without doubt, a Paradox
The Ground is volatile, with aftershocks
Held in this Prison eternally.....
Forever in an emotional Perjury

What I Am

I am the conscious consciousness
I am one becoming a whole
I am the Earth becoming Space
I am me, becoming you
I am nothing, becoming something
I am the unreal becoming real
I am Human, yet I am an Alien
I am the Sea, that becomes the Ocean
I am a Whisper, becoming a Shout
I am Love becoming unloved
I am a Child, that became a Mother
I am peaceful, yet far from serene
I am this and I will be that
I am perfect through imperfection
I am bad but still so good
I am bored but still passionate
I am the now, that becomes hindsight
I am experience, that becomes foresight
I am not much, yet I am enough
I am unfeeling, yet can be unfeeling
I am beautiful yet, become so ugly
I am a treasure that becomes too lost
How can I be all this, but be all that?

My God

know you are there,
But I do wonder
When life isn't fair
......into the yonder

All this pain & suffering
Prayers get silently said
Yet no comfort do you bring
To this misery, I seem wed

Feel like saying 'Fuck you'
Though, I must not blaspheme you lord
But, do you have any clue?
With all the lives you seem to afford?

Politicians know Sweet F.A
Who, do we have to turn to?
You know, make things better & OK?
It seems a very cruel God, that's who!

A full circle turned, from all the Hate
To this feeling of 'needing' to believe
A vision of Heaven, I anticipate
To one day go, when it's time to leave

You

I have fallen in your estimation
Accepting, of your damnation
But, briefly before you leave
let me tell you then I'll grieve
whether the flirting was meaningless
is an answer that I could only guess
the staring and looks that you gave
I will take with me, to the grave
but I ask, if its guilt you can taste?
maybe its deception based
resentful of me for your feelings
perhaps I am Right, you are a weakling
there are pictures of us together
smiling, I will continue to treasure
we look in some like a couple
but your hate has burst that bubble
I loved you, 'conian please
yes now, your heart can freeze
it was an affair of the heart
nothing more, we were smart
on that note, I blow you a kiss
Our times together, I will miss

I wanted

I wanted to take you to the Stars
Walk on The Moon & skip on Mars
Just one touch of the much needed fate
Out of time, crucially much too late
I feel you when you are thinking
Of me, our Minds are one & linking
Don't try to push me away, resist
Hold me near, in the Cloudy Midst
Feel the warmth of my Body
Let me worship, for you are Godly
Everything you want & so need
Come into me & on my Love feed
Stay as one, let me feel you all night
Slow, take your time & don't fight
Let The Planets align for us, one time
Everything that is past, it will rhyme
Let me see your unseen Dimension
I want to resolve this unwanted tension
Let me lay in your arms, in the afterglow
Resting, I watch you inhale & then blow
We will not meet again in this lifetime
Fading Shooting Stars, still in their prime

My Falling

No longer on your Friends List
I get the feeling, you are pissed
You had better listen & listen good
I couldn't help falling for you Bud
You have shut me off completely
Compartmentalised me neatly
I assume, it's me you dislike
Too honest maybe, I am no Bike
No others have compared to you
They simply don't fill your Shoes
I am not bitter, but I'm Heartbroken
I don't play Games, I'm outspoken
I wish you would tell me what I've done
It's this that is destroying me Hun
I will love you always, from afar
But, your Friend I am, how bizarre
This is a new experience for me
All of it, to wanting so quietly
I, wish you nothing but happiness
Your Wife too, may God Bless
No wrong has been done
But, my Mind has been run
So, please watch me walk away
To hopefully, find another you someday.

It's Dirty

This hurts, but it's going to hurt first
These times in mind, come in short burst
They happen, between times in Life
Piercing my beating Heart, like a Knife
I know, I keep coming back for more
This is another of my annoying flaws
....for which I can only say 'sorry'
But, feel beaten by a seven ton lorry
I am drowning, under Love's vicious Waves
It's just forgiveness, is all I crave
Not your touch and not your smile
They are nice, but I get bored after a while
This is deeper than that and dirtier
Fleeting in time, muddy and spongier
I accept that we cannot and will not ever be
Though, please smile, just forgive me.

Why?

How do I go on from this?
"It was an unplanned Kiss"
Am I not worthy of loyalty?
I'm not asking to be royalty
Must be me, yes, it must
Why, did they break my trust?
I am broken and in pieces, torn
My Partner, faithful, I mourn
I cannot stop these Tears
Almost self pitying, it appears
What to do now?, I just don't know
...and what of our love, where will it go?
Shocked, yes, shocked to the core
I simply cannot take it any more
Voices stuck on replay, I cover my Ears
Just, right here, let me disappear
Time, yes, time I need aplenty
I am feeling so old & wish I was Twenty
My life, is now in tatters, I feel
Once more to Sleep, over I keel

High

The music *is* undoubtedly soothing
I am a God, over seeing & ruling
The body has gone, disappeared
All that remains, should be feared
The power of thought is undermined
The Stars have undeniably aligned
A Master of my own built Europa
Sensorially high on Levodopa
The sound in my head is magnified
A Solar System explodes, petrified
You by me, is all I desire & need
On your energy, let me feed
Through the quiet of the Night, I fly
Replacing all the lost Stars in the Sky
Awakening from a maddening Sleep
I ask, that my broken Soul, you keep.

Ethereal

Upon my Death, I will reunite
With you at my close right
I will be the unconditional Love
The ever pure, White eternal Dove
I have learnt from Life's lesson's
The fine hand picked Delicatessens
Through the Clouds, we will ride
Ascending to position, Spirit Guide
All that we ever were & so will be
Is here, proudly, with me....
An ethereal cord is attached
For we are so perfectly matched
Set adrift on a memory bliss....
& sealing Eternity with a Kiss.

I Am Guilty

I have died another Death
Made Love with another
Taken, its seems, final breath
Our Bodies, entwined....
& our Souls they danced
The Deal is now signed
But what happens now?
Will the guilt tear us part?
....Our Bodies made a Vow
Sex has grown into Love
You are what I want...
when push comes to shove
Hearts will break & tears spill
Are we worth so much?
Being without you, I chill
I need to think about this
Morally & financially...
It's an expensive kind of bliss
We could carry on a lie
With our current Partner...
We could grieve & cry...
Guilt will come between us
Reputations will be damaged
Was it worth all this fuss?

Gin

My troubles, while alive in reality
Transcended with me, to immortality
Alive, I could not cope any more
Easy! I would walk thru' Death's Door
Of course, I felt bad for my Family
Tears, they said "I wasn't Manly"
It wasn't their fault, they couldn't win
My only solace, was in a Bottle of Gin
In my Pit of Despair, my only option
Was to put sober me, up for adoption
Around a Green Table, I would play Cards
Waiting to win & Lucifer would guard
He wanted everything in between
Everything good, I was the unclean
Anything that could make me see
The Gin Bottle took away from me
I am in permanent despair & lonely
Death is dark, dank & ungodly
I'm still very depressed, sod me!
You would imagine, I am at peace now
Ironic, shake my Head & raise the brow
I will not encourage another illusion
So selflessly, I refuse Alcohol's infusion
Never feel bad for how I turned out
Or Event's you knew nothing about
Without Gin, I can hold my Hands up
It's my fault, drinking from Lucifer's Cup.

Poetry

Without Poetry is there Synchronicity?
Without Synchonicity, would there be Spirituality?
Without Spirituality, would there be a God?
Without a God, would there be a purpose?
Without a purpose, would I be here?
Without me, would there be a World?
Without a World, would there be a you?
Without you, would there be this?
Without this, would there even be a question?

Come Here

Beckoning you for a Kiss
From slightly parted Lips
The warmth of our Breath
Makes me high like Meth
A heartfelt rising passion
Like, its going out of Fashion
Our Souls, are now moving
Dancing, silently Grooving
Singing the unsaid words
Frequently sung by Birds
Fall, into a warm dark Hole
Colours of the blackest Coal
Saved by the softest devotion
Caressed by sweet explosion
A parting & smile in the Eye's
A wetness, between the Thighs

Fooled

I fell into a false sense of Security
Within our Friendship's maturity
It was forbidden land & bad terrain
I realise now, as I feel such pain
My Fingers got burnt, badly blistered
Pieces of my Heart, torn & littered
Release your choke & let me breathe
You are burying me, I see you seethe
A disdain in your words, almost a shame
Chosen carefully, to add, a harsh aim
I sense some disgust, that I dare fall
For you, who was already on call
My Love was real, it had deepened
To you, I know, I have cheapened
Residing in 'ignore me Land'
I now talk to the Palm of your Hand
I do wish to talk to your Face
Hang on, my Heart has to now pace
I would have been unfaithful with you
I am sorry if this alters your prior view.

My Ego & I

I would like to introduce my Ego to you
It's often seen grazing among the Dusk Dew
I think of it, as perhaps slim and youthful
Though, the truth of it, is somewhat brutal
I see and feel more than I quite often say
Empathic, for better and worse, it's OK
There are times, when the 'Watcher' gatecrashes
Then, they become one and the Plane crashes
I have to remember to separate my good self
Sometimes, even put the Ego upon the Shelf
The Watcher is good and all grown up
The Ego, irresponsible and quite corrupt
I have reached that age, where I know
That my Ego comes second, belongs on tow
It's happy, even if sometimes threatened
By the Watcher, but it's never lessened
The Watcher wears Doc Martin's
It has attitude with two Chins
These things, help make me who I am
So, criticise me. I don't give a damn!

Day Into Night

Take my Hand & into the Night, let's run
Where we will watch the setting of The Sun
The Sun fades & makes way for The Night
While The Moon smiles & wins a silent Fight
The Evening takes on a damp & misty coolness
It's clear, that The Earth is in a state of undress
The Stars, they shine. One by one
The Sun was here, but now it's gone
The length of our Day is over so fast
When Day light surrenders, at half past
In the darkness of these coming hours
Dreams are dreamt, as the Moon Dust scours
Resting upon The Grass, The Morning Dew
Then, its the break of a new day, just for you

Meet Me

Broken thoughts & fragmented Sleep
About Enemies & High Towered Forts
Waving a White Flag in Surrender
am down in perfect Battle splendour
It's tragic we cannot return to Friend
That I am in 'ignore me land' to the end
I hunger for just a smile or a handshake
Everything & nothing, I will so make
Why do you knowingly avoid my Eyes?
I am tired of your lies on hurtful lies
Lies you pass has ignorant bliss....
...I'm sorry you know, you don't miss
My Hands are held in retreat, high
Bleeding on the inside, refusing to cry
Meet me in the middle, held out hand
Once more, let's make this Holy Land.

Panic

My Mind proceeds to play this cheap trick
Haunting visions, that make me feel sick
Slow motion imagery, of Black and White
Grappling with insanity, I am OK. Alright.
Those last Words when you turned away
They grasp at my Heart, stuck on replay
An urge to vomit, while I try to call.....
I fall to my Knees, I have to crawl
The Ground pulls me down, it's defying
Lucifer laughs at my thoughts, he's prying
I wonder if you are happy, these days...
While faced with Concrete, I meet your gaze
It was a long way down with Gravity....
To feeling so low, oh the harsh depravity.

Primal Fear

LIKE A MOTH TO A FLAME
WILD, A LION THAT'S UNTAMED
PREDATORY & NOW HUNTED
EVEN WHEN YOU ARE CONFRONTED
PLEAD TO ME YOUR INNOCENCE
THE SOUND OF DISSONANCE
BACKED INTO AN UNSAFE PLACE
I KNOW I HAVE TOUCHED BASE
IT'S ENOUGH FOR ME TO BE ALIVE
TO HAVE EXISTED, AN ARCHIVE
I LOOK AT YOU CHALLENGINGLY
IN THE EYES, NOW TALK TO ME
OPEN YOUR HEART & MIND
CLOSE YOUR EYES, SPEAK BLIND
USE ONLY YOUR PRIMAL INSTINCT
FOR WE, YOU KNOW ARE LINKED
MY CONTEMPT IS IN YOUR EYE'S
IT'S YOURS & OPENLY DEFIES
ANY YOU HAVE GIVEN ME FIRST
I CAN SMELL DESIRE, YOUR THIRST
IT'S ENOUGH THAT I HAVE POWER
SO MUCH, TO MAKE YOU COWER
I HUNGER NOW FOR MUCH MORE
FOR A KING, WITH A LOUDER ROAR

My Harsh Reality

Blood seeps from The Crown, worn
From the odd misplaced Thorn
Tears you cry, full of misplaced Pity
You Father sacrificed you, didn't he?
With much emotion, he convinced me
That you are a figment of imagination
Full of controversial bullshit & sensation
Created with intelligence & such evil
From Brain's the size of Boll Weevil's
We are Children of one God, a belief
Inflicted with our own Cross, a relief
My Brother's & Sister's, perhaps
Your Christianity sadly collapsed
These are my words & my beliefs
It is your Government, that are Thieves
It is they, that you are worshipping
A governed religion, of home shipping
The Government worships your Satan
I know, smite me down with a Baton
Your Religion & your God are challenged
I will 'stand Trial' for the alleged

A Suggestion

If I stay in the background
It will be easy yet complex
A pleasing arrangement
Would it, I wonder be allowed?
It's not Black and White I know
There is this smidgeon of Grey
There is a Fire burning within
Simmering, on the down low
What is on your intelligent Mind
I'm curious as to what you are thinking?
I see a Man, enjoying my company
Gentleman, a flirt and always kind
They won't go away, thoughts filthy
Of Body and Mind, vivid and raw
A forbidden Fruit, The Snake beckons
....Right now....I'm not.....guilty

Self Harm

A fleeting pain, I tremble & fall to my Knees
I can only mouth for help, while my arms bleed
I have felt what it is to feel, with my Mind
An invisible emotion, that is real & very unkind

With every cut, I see you smile & clap
Finding pleasure immensely, I fall into your Trap
Most entertaining, for you who set it
I am crying, I am chomping at the bit

Curling into a Ball, shivering and on the Floor
I make the decision not to be controlled any more
No more will I beg for your attention or love
I will not be yours to abuse, play with or shove

Attracted

You strip me bare of my Ego
I am hopeless, this I do know
Don't walk towards me
I can't look at you. See?
There is a certainty in you
In quietness, all you do

I can't see The Crucifix you wear
It's more than I can really bear
Close isn't possible, I'm afraid
I'm edging around a Grenade
What if you see how I feel?
Crush me underfoot & Heel

You got me feeling vulnerable
Something I am not comfortable
The Heart is full of definite Scars
Of past Loves, I shared with Stars
Lonely times have served me well
When there is only the Skies, to tell

Stop reading me with your Eyes
It's not fair that you see previous Lies
Can't see past the warning sign
But still the scent of Bodies, entwine
The red embers of the Fire, the Smoke

Need to get away, find personal space
Be alone, disengage from The Rat Race
I didn't realise, I had begun to perspire
Clearly I'm not meant to be close to the Fire
I am ageing and breaking down on my own
I will spend the rest of my day's alone

I

The LAST GOODBYE

EACH PLAYED THEIR PART IN THIS
I AM BLOWING YOU A SOFT KISS
TEARS BORN OF FRUSTRATION
FROM SOMETHING, OUR CREATION
WHISPERS OF US STILL FLOATING
WITHOUT THEIR SUGAR-COATING
YOU WILL ALWAYS BE IN DENIAL
JUST AS I WILL BE 'ON TRIAL'
FENCE ME UP & CHAIN ME IN
FOR NO CRIME, OR REAL SIN
I WILL SHOULDER THE BURDEN &...
TAKE THE BLAME FROM YOUR HAND
I WILL CARRY ON BEING A NOTHING
THAT WAS OBVIOUSLY SOMETHING
WITH A REGRETFUL BYE & WAVE
NO LONGER, WILL I BE YOUR SLAVE
THE TIES & THREADS ARE CUT
A SPARE ROOM, IN THE CORNER PUT
I WILL IN TIME, THINK OF YOU FONDLY
THOUGH RIGHT NOW, IT'S BEYOND ME.

Goodbye x

Lightning Source UK Ltd.
Milton Keynes UK
UKHW011314090119

335271UK00009B/627/P